CULTURE ENCYCLOPEDIA

DESIGN

CULTURE ENCYCLOPEDIA

DESIGN

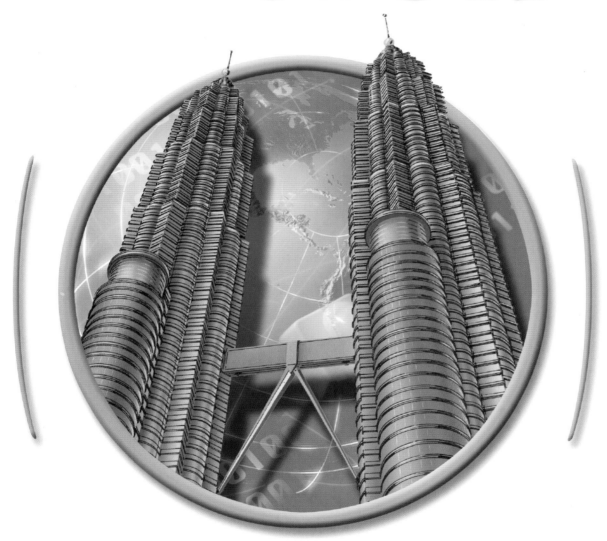

Fiona MacDonald

Miles Kelly

PUBLISHING

First published in 2002 by
Miles Kelly Publishing Ltd
The Bardfield Centre
Great Bardfield
Essex CM7 4SL

2 4 6 8 10 9 7 5 3 1

Author
Fiona MacDonald

Designed and Edited by
Starry Dog Books

Project Editor
Belinda Gallagher

Assistant Editors
Mark Darling, Nicola Jessop, Isla Macuish

Artwork Commissioning
Lesley Cartlidge

Indexer
Jane Parker

Picture Research
Ruth Boardman, Liberty Newton

Colour Reproduction
DPI Colour, Saffron Walden, Essex

ISBN 1-84236-224-0

Printed in China

A British Library Cataloguing-in-Publication Data
A catalogue record for this book is available from the British Library

www.mileskelly.net
info@mileskelly.net

Contents

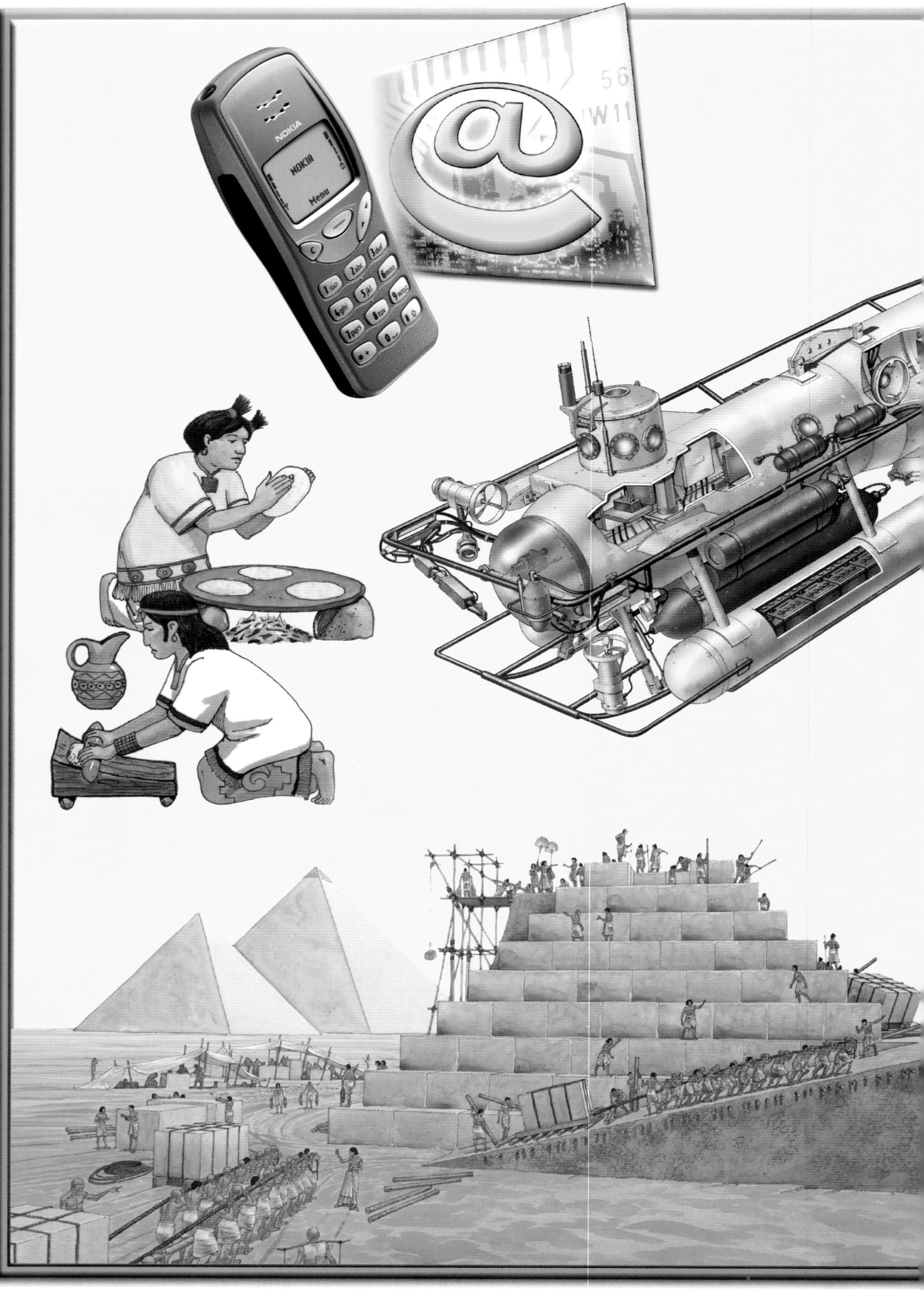
NOKIA
NOKIA
Menu
56
W11

Design

OBJECTS that are planned and made for a particular purpose are described as being 'designed'. The word is most frequently used in connection with fashion, architecture, computers and publishing. But design also forms an important part of most manufacturing and engineering processes. A designer combines problem-solving with creativity and precise attention to detail. Today, the word 'designer' is often used to suggest that items are of good quality, and in the latest, exclusive style. But in the past, there were many discussions and disagreements about what made 'good' design.

Many kinds of design

WE ARE surrounded by examples of 'design'. But they often have very different origins. Some are so old that we do not know who invented them. They have changed in detail over thousands of years, but their essential structure and function is the same. Others are based on old ideas, but have been modified by the discovery of new materials, or scientific techniques. Some exclusive designs are still handmade in traditional style. For the past 200 years, many designs have been shaped by the processes used to make them. Today, most designed items combine cheapness of manufacture with popular mass-market appeal.

◪ NATIONAL SYMBOL

Currency notes are designed as a sign of national identity, and, often, pride. They are decorated with easily recognizable national symbols such as portraits of national heroes or famous landmarks.

◨ USEFUL OR BEAUTIFUL?

For centuries, people have questioned whether a well-designed object is simply one that is good to look at, or whether it should be practical as well. Traditional blacksmiths tried to combine usefulness with attractive designs when making simple tools and iron fastenings.

◪ HIGH RISE

The first 'skyscrapers' were built in the late 19th century. Originally they were designed to make the best use of limited space at ground level, as well as to look impressive. But critics claim that skyscrapers can be lonely places in which to live, and that they cause 'visual pollution'.

OLD OR NEW?

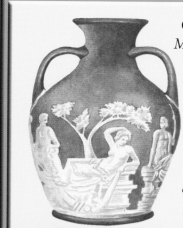

Many designers strive to be original, while others borrow from the past. In the 18th and 19th centuries, British vase designers were influenced by the art of ancient Rome, creating similar styles of their own.

☑ INDIVIDUAL STYLE

Some designers win fame for their personal style. The Spanish architect Antonio Gaudi (1853–1926) is famous for his original and unusual building designs. Most of his buildings are in the city of Barcelona in Spain. In an attempt to break away from historical styles, he used flowing curves in many of his buildings, which he decorated with brightly coloured ceramics or mosaics of glass.

◪ MASS-PRODUCED

From the 19th century onward, millions of identical items were made by machines in factories. Mass-production allowed people to buy attractive, practical goods more cheaply than ever before. Before mass-production, tools, clothes, furniture and household items were all made slowly and carefully by hand, and were often very expensive.

☑ SAFETY FIRST

Bridges are some of the biggest and most beautiful structures in the world. But their graceful curves and arches are the result of careful mathematical calculations, not simply 'artistic' design. Their strength and safety are more important than their appearance.

Who designs?

EVERYTHING that is made – by hand or by machine – is the result of a decision. Someone, somewhere, has decided to paint, carve, sew, assemble or construct it using particular materials and a specific plan. Some objects are the result of long years of tradition. Their original shape, size, or component parts may have been adapted or improved over the centuries. More recent objects are often created either as experiments, to set fashion trends, to meet an urgent need or just for fun. The designers' names are generally known, and they may even be celebrities, particularly if they design clothes.

◪ TOOLS FOR THE JOB

One of the earliest-designed tools was the stone axe, made for cutting. This one was made about 8000 BC. Stone axes helped bring about a revolution in food production. The earliest farmers used them to chop down trees and clear land so they could grow crops.

◪ FAMOUS ARTISTS

For thousands of years, artists have been employed to create beautiful paintings and sculptures to bring glory to rich nations or powerful families. This stone carving was made by Phidias, the most famous sculptor in ancient Greece, about 430 BC. It decorated the Parthenon, a splendid temple in Athens.

◪ DESIGNED BY SCRIBES

Ancient Egypt's pyramids, the giant tombs of the pharaohs (kings), were designed by scribes – well-educated writers from each pharaoh's court. They were built by people who normally farmed the land.

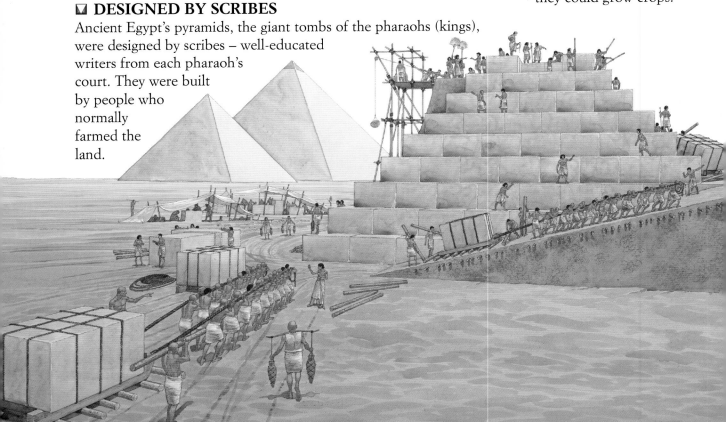

MASTER MASONS

During the Middle Ages (c. AD 1000–1500), master masons designed and built magnificent cathedrals in many European cities. On the plaster floors of their 'drawing-rooms' they drew detailed plans for stone windows and arches.

◧ SKILL AND CALCULATION

Design is often a matter of artistic flair combined with rigorous mechanical calculation. Both are essential to create an object that looks good and functions well. Great sailing ships, like these shown in an 18th-century dockyard, looked beautiful. But their design was also carefully calculated to keep them afloat, carry loads and sail fast.

◧ LIVING IN STYLE

People have always liked their surroundings to reflect their artistic tastes and sense of style. Some pay for experts, called 'interior designers' to design their homes. Others consult books, magazines and TV programmes for new decorative ideas. This design for a family drawing room was published in a British magazine in 1884.

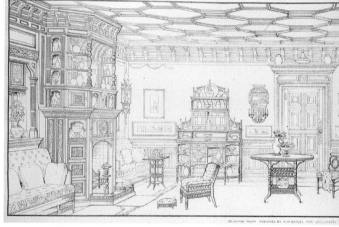

◧ DESIGNS FOR KNOWLEDGE

During the late 20th century, designers emerged in the new field of 'information technology' (IT). Some specialized in electronics, telecommunications or computer hardware. Others created web sites with sounds and moving pictures, or devised specialized software for scientists like this oceanographer.

Houses and furnishings

ALL around the word, people's basic housing needs are the same. They want a home that will provide shelter from heat or cold, somewhere comfortable to eat and sleep, and protection from intruders or enemies. Many different designs have developed to meet these needs. Today's homes are often built from factory-made materials such as concrete, plastic, steel and tinted glass. In the past, builders had to use local supplies of materials such as wood, clay or stone, as it was too difficult – and costly – to transport them long distances. Home furnishings are often status symbols. Rich people may choose exclusive, luxurious designs as a sign of wealth and power. Poor people have to survive in much smaller, often crowed homes that may not have clean water, heating or power supplies.

◤ MALI MOUNTAIN HOMES

The Dogon people of Mali, in Africa, design their villages in the shape of the first woman created by God, to reflect their religious beliefs. The men's meeting house is her head, groups of family homes are her body, and women's private rooms are her hands.

◤ FAMILY VALUES

In 1895, the sitting room of a moderately wealthy family in America was designed to provide a comfortable living space for a large number of people. Painting, reading, sewing, letter writing and conversation were usual pastimes, but everything was kept neat and tidy, reflecting the shared family values.

◀ OLD AND NEW

Ideas about design change rapidly over time. They change with fashion, developing technology, and with new ideas about the best way to live. Big cities often reveal great contrasts between old and new housing designs. In Singapore, for example, these traditional low-rise, decorated houses are dwarfed by modern high-rise apartments.

◪ MODERN LIVING

In the late 20th century, kitchens were filled with all kinds of functional, but unattractive, electric-powered devices such as refrigerators, dishwashers and microwave ovens. Homeowners concealed them in specially designed, matching cupboards like these. Today, many appliances have become 'designer' items, and the fashion is to display them.

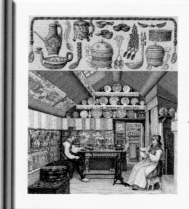

FOREST HOMES
Traditionally, Scandinavian homes like this Swedish house were built of pine wood from the nearby forests. Furniture, tools and utensils were also made of pine, often painted with bright designs.

◪ FOR CITY MERCHANTS

In crowded cities, where there is not much space for building, houses are often built several storeys high and closely packed together, to fit in as many people as possible. These tall merchants' houses in Amsterdam, in the Netherlands, were designed about 1650. They were built beside one of the city's many canals, which were used by cargo boats. Some houses had cranes in the roof to haul goods up to attic store rooms. Today, waterside houses are often the most desirable, both for homeowners and tourists alike.

◪ UNDER ONE ROOF

In many parts of the world, extended families live together under one roof. On the Southeast Asian island of Sumatra, in Indonesia, for example, the Batak people live in large family groups in decorated wooden houses. The floor of the building is supported on wooden posts at head-height, and is covered by a tall, curved roof that ends in two points, like buffalo horns. Traditionally the houses were held together with wooden pins instead of nails.

DESIGN

Big buildings

WHY do architects design big buildings, and wealthy families or businesses pay for them? Over the centuries there has been one main reason – to impress. Other reasons include political pride and love. Temples and cathedrals were built as places of worship. Arenas were centres for sport. Castles and forts were built to control lords' lands, and great tombs were built as memorials to people who were respected or loved. Public monuments display national pride, while today's huge modern office blocks proclaim a company's – or a city's – wealth, power and confidence.

◩ MYSTERIOUS STONEHENGE
Stonehenge is a massive prehistoric monument in southwest England. The circular bank and ditch, and the three stone circles within them, were built in stages between about 3000 and 1500 BC. No one knows exactly why Stonehenge was built, but it was probably designed as a temple.

☑ THE GREATEST ROMAN AMPHITHEATRE
The Colosseum in Rome, Italy, was the greatest amphitheatre, or circular arena, built by the ancient Romans. It was constructed from an early form of concrete. Completed in AD 80, it was designed to hold 50,000 spectators, who went there to watch bloodthirsty gladiator fights and battles between men and wild animals.

wooden seats for
women at the top

posts for
awning

tiered seats
for men

sand-covered arena

outer
corridors

underground cages

■ MIGHTY CASTLES

Castles were among the biggest buildings in the world before about AD 1800. The earliest castles were built from wood about AD 900, as shelters for soldiers. They developed over the next 300 years into huge stone buildings like this one. More than 20,000 stood in Britain, France and Germany.

■ THE SERENE TAJ MAHAL

The marble Taj Mahal in Agra, India, is one of the largest and most beautiful tombs in the world. Completed about AD 1648, it houses the body of Mumtaz Mahal, wife of Emperor Shah Jahan, who ruled the Mughal empire from 1628 to 1658.

■ THE EIFFEL TOWER

The 300-metre-high Eiffel Tower in Paris, France, was completed in 1889 to mark the centenary of the French Revolution of 1789. It was made of wrought iron, a new material for structures or buildings at that time.

glass-covered bridge at 50th floor

■ PETRONAS TOWERS

The twin concrete, glass and steel Petronas Towers in Kuala Lumpur, Malaysia, are 88 storeys high and are topped by spires. Each floor is shaped like an eight-pointed star.

TALLEST BUILDINGS

PETRONAS 1 AND 2
Kuala Lumpur, Malaysia
449 metres   1998

SEARS TOWER
Chicago, Illinois
439 metres   1974

JIN MAO BUILDING
Shanghai, China
418 metres   1998

CITIC PLAZA
Guangzhou, China
389 metres   1996

SHUN HING SQUARE
Shenzhen, China
382 metres   1996

EMPIRE STATE BUILDING
New York City
379 metres   1931

CENTRAL PLAZA
Hong Kong
372 metres   1992

BANK OF CHINA
Hong Kong
366 metres   1989

EMIRATES TOWERS
Dubai, UAE
353 metres   1999

THE CENTRE
Hong Kong, CHINA
348 metres   1998

Early tools and machines

Humans are the only species on Earth to deliberately design tools and machines to help them with all aspects of their lives. The name 'tool' is usually given to objects designed to perform a specific task, such as hammering or chopping. The word 'machine' is more often used to describe a larger, more complicated object, driven by some kind of motor, rather than human muscle-power. Tools for everyday tasks, such as knives, are usually simple, straightforward and easy to make, as well as easy to use. In contrast, tools and machines for precise purposes, or for tasks that need to be repeated, are often complex in design. Their construction needs special skills.

▨ CUTTING AND DIGGING
About 2.5 million years ago, early humans began to make tools by chipping stones to create a sharp edge. Later Stone Age tools, like this flint hand axe (c.100,000 BC), were designed for cutting up dead animals or digging up edible roots.

▨ LIFTING POWER
Cranes are machines that are designed to lift heavy loads. By 1900, ironworks like this one in Germany were using huge beam cranes to move red-hot iron bars from the furnace to the steam-powered hammer, which hit them into shape.

▨ ANIMAL POWER
For thousands of years, people designed ways of harnessing animal power to help them in their work. Before motorized ploughs were invented, farmers used horse-drawn ploughs to cultivate their fields. Horses wearing padded collars, to cushion the load, were able to pull an iron-tipped plough share through heavy ground.

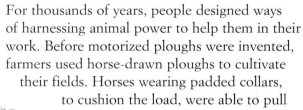

☑ STEAM ENGINE

Machines powered by steam revolutionized industry in the 19th century. They made all kinds of goods more quickly and cheaply than old-style machines worked by hand. This massive steam engine powered machines in factories in the north of Britain. It was fuelled by coal from the plentiful local mines, and water from the hill streams.

☑ A SCIENTIST'S INSTRUMENT

Tools are used by a person to do a task, whereas instruments provide information. The microscope is an instrument used by scientists to study objects too small to be seen with the naked eye. It was invented in the 17th century. This one was used by Robert Hooke (1635–1703), who first identified cells – the basic building blocks of all living things.

☑ POWER FROM RIVERS AND STREAMS

Water-wheels were probably invented in the Middle East. They have been used for more than 2000 years both to raise water and to harness the power of flowing water to drive machinery. Before the invention of the steam engine in the 1700s, water-wheels were used to power mills, where grain was ground into flour. As water flowed over the paddles on the wheel, it turned the wheel, which then rotated two flat grindstones that crushed the grain.

SCISSORS

Scissors are a cutting tool made from two blades, each with a handle, and joined by a screw in the middle. One handle slips over a finger and the other over the thumb. If the handles are pushed apart, the blades open, and when pulled together, they close with a cutting action. Scissors of bronze or iron were first used in ancient China and Japan, as well as by the Romans. But from 1761, they were cast in steel and mass-produced in England.

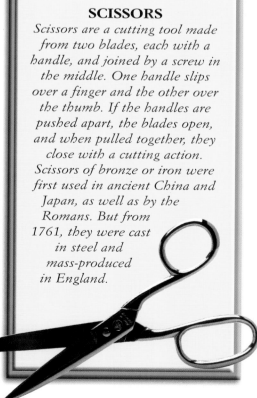

DESIGN

New technologies

FROM about AD 1750, tools and machines were designed by professional scientists, inventors, and engineers. They were made from 'modern' manufactured materials, such as metal alloys (mixtures), in the 19th century, and plastics in the 20th century. Scientific discoveries such as X-rays and jet propulsion allowed inventors to create new technology for medicine, engineering and information handling. Many 21st-century machines no longer need humans to operate them. Instead, they can perform tasks by themselves, and even make simple decisions. Some people predict that, before long, inventors will design a new race of 'cyborgs' – part machine, part human.

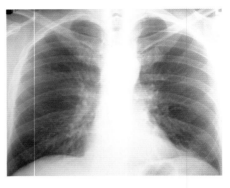

◪ X-RAY VISION
In 1895, X-rays, which allow us to 'see through' substances, were discovered. They are widely used in medicine to diagnose illness, and in engineering to search for hidden cracks and flaws.

◪ JET-PROPELLED
Jet engines work by compressing and burning oil vapour and air, then pushing out exhaust gases. They were invented in the 1930s by designers Whittle (in Britain) and von Ohain (in Germany). In the late 20th century, aircraft powered by jet engines made air travel quicker and less expensive than ever before.

◪ INSIDE STORY
CAT scanners use X-rays to view 'slices' or cross-sections, of organs inside a person's body. These are presented on a computer screen as digital images for doctors to look at and examine for illness. 'CAT' stands for 'Computerized Axial Tomography' a process first used about 1980.

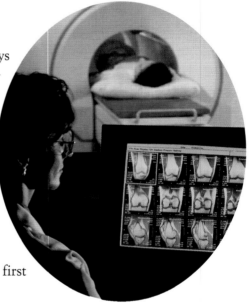

◪ NATURE POWER
Wind power has been used to drive simple machines for centuries, but in the 20th century, engineers invented machines to generate electricity from wind power. Today, many countries, especially in northern Europe, use wind power to generate electricity, instead of making it by burning fossil fuels. It is inexpensive and non-polluting, but noisy.

☑ BLAST OFF!

Rockets were one of the most important machines of the 20th century. Without them, astronauts would not have been able to leave Earth and travel in space. Like jets, rockets are propelled by burning gas. But they also carry a substance called an oxidizer, which allows their engines to operate in space, where there is no air. Simple rockets, fuelled by gunpowder, were made in China about AD 1300. Modern rockets were pioneered by Russian engineer Konstantin Tsiolkovsky (1857–1935). His ideas were later developed in the United States and the former Soviet Union.

COMPUTERS

Computers were originally designed as machines to store and process data. Today, life would be impossible without them for many people. Smaller, and more affordable than ever before, they are used by organizations as diverse as governments and children's play groups.

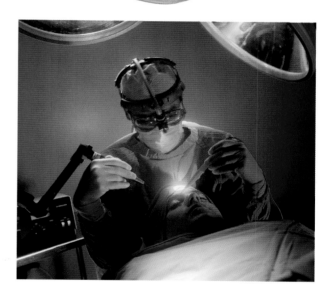

◪ LASER SURGERY

Lasers are machines that produce intense beams of high-energy light. They can melt, burn, or cut through many different substances, from metals to human bodies, and are often used for delicate surgery. They can also be used to make precise measurements, in printing, to guide weapons, and to read supermarket bar codes. Lasers were first built in 1960 by American Theodore Maiman (b. 1927).

Designs for food

FOOD is essential for survival. It can also symbolize love, friendship and happiness. Throughout the past, people have invented ways of cooking raw foodstuffs to make them safe and tasty to eat, and have designed technologies for storing, processing, cooking and serving many different kinds of meat, fish and edible plants. Professional cooks (usually men) and family carers (usually women) have prepared meals to suit many different needs – from fast-food snacks that provide instant body-fuel and satisfy hunger, to elaborate meals that welcome guests and celebrate special occasions.

◁ MAKING OIL

In ancient Greece and Rome, ripe olives were harvested from trees every year and crushed in large wooden presses to extract a rich, fragrant oil. This was used in cooking, cleaning and beauty care, just as it is today.

◩ WELL-TRAINED STAFF

From about AD 1000–1600, wealthy families living in castles employed a large staff of well-trained cooks and kitchen boys, or scullions, to prepare and cook food for them and their guests. Cooking technology was simple. Meat was roasted on spits over huge open fires, or stewed in large metal cauldrons; the basic kitchen tools were knives and spoons.

◪ MADE BY HAND

In the 16th century, Aztec women from Mexico ground maize between stones to make flour and mixed it with water to form dough. They rolled and shaped the dough into tortillas – thin, flat pancakes – and baked them on a heated stone. Tortillas were the Aztecs' basic food.

◀ LOOKING GOOD

Japanese cooks are famous for their skill at arranging food, carefully combining different colours, shapes and textures on the plate. Food that looks good can be a 'feast for the eyes'. Like the smell of good cooking, attractive food increases the appetite and tempts people to eat. Presenting food well also shows respect for the people to whom it is offered.

▷ WELL-PRESERVED

Methods of food preservation were devised hundreds of years ago. People preserved meat and fish by smoking it, drying it or storing it in barrels of salt, as shown here. All three methods kill the bacteria, or germs, that live inside the food. If not preserved, food left at room temperature will begin to decay as the bacteria multiply. Food containing too much harmful bacteria may make people ill, and can even kill them.

COOKING BY RADIO?

Invented in about 1953, microwave ovens use very short radio waves to heat food and cook it. As the radio waves pass through the food, they 'excite' all the molecules of liquid in the food, making the liquid hot. The heat spreads quickly through the food.

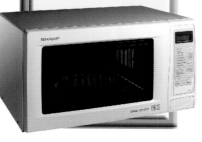

▷ CHILLING!

Storing food at low temperatures stops dangerous bacteria from growing, and can keep fruit and vegetables crisp and fresh. Traditionally, food was kept cool in cupboards or small rooms called 'larders'. Refrigerators were invented by American engineer John Gorrie (1803–55) in 1851, and were more reliable. Freezers first appeared in 1929, invented by American businessman Clarence Birdseye (1886–1956). Today, most homes in developed countries have both. Large refrigerated trucks carry chilled or frozen foods from factories direct to the shops to sell.

Clothes and fashion

CLOTHES do more than keep us warm. They also display our wealth, status, and, sometimes, our occupation. If they are traditional in style, they may reveal which part of the world we come from, and which faith we follow. If they are unusual, we may wear them as a sign of rebellion, or to show that we belong to a special group. The first clothes ever made were sewn from animal skins and furs about 70,000 years ago. Since then, people have designed clothes, jewellery and make-up in many different styles. Today, designer fashion is big business.

◩ BEADS AND FEATHERS

In Papua New Guinea, men attend traditional religious ceremonies wearing face paint and feather headdresses. Ornaments on clothing, traditionally made from feathers, shells and stones, date back over a million years. All over the world, specially designed clothes decorated with extra ornaments are worn for special occasions, such as getting married.

◪ TEXTILE REVOLUTION

The ancient Egyptians wore clothes made of linen, woven from fibres of the flax plant. Long, horizontal looms were used to weave the cloth. About 1500 BC, a new cloth-making technology arrived in Egypt from the Middle East. Expert weavers began to make patterned tapestries from woollen thread on big, upright looms.

◪ HANDMADE FOOTWEAR

Until the late 19th century, boots, and shoes were made by hand. The cobbler, who was both a shoemaker and mender, cut pieces of leather to make the tops, or uppers, and soles. He fitted these over a foot-shaped model, called a last, and joined them together with stitches or tiny nails.

☑ THE LATEST FASHIONS

Until the 19th century, ordinary people knew little about the new fashions of the rich, or foreign styles. Fashion plates (hand-coloured engravings) spread the news of the latest trends – these dresses were designed in 1883. Paper patterns in magazines and the invention of sewing machines also made fashions more widely available.

COCO CHANEL

Gabrielle 'Coco' Chanel (1883–1971) created a whole new style of clothing for women based on simple designs, often using square shapes. By the 1930s, she was the richest designer in France.

☑ BIG BUSINESS

By the 20th century, designer fashion had become big business. Although world-famous models paraded elegantly down catwalks to display exclusive, handmade garments to wealthy customers, most fashion designers made money from selling cheap, mass-made copies of 'ready-to-wear' collections, or by licensing everyday clothes such as jeans, which were labelled with their names.

☑ BACKSTRAP LOOM

The backstrap loom was invented about 4000 years ago. Lightweight, cheap and portable, it is still used by many peoples around the world, including the Apa Tani of northeast India. The weaver ties one end of the loom around his or her waist, and fastens the other end to a post. Leaning backward keeps the threads at the correct tension for weaving. Narrow lengths of fabric are woven, and are used to make clothes for the weaver's family.

Communications

THE earliest means of communication were visual. People used hand gestures and signs. These were soon joined by grunts and other simple sounds, which in time became words. Spoken languages developed, using many words and complicated grammar, which gave the languages their structure. As soon as languages were first written down, design became an essential part of communication. Today, movies, television, the Internet, newspapers, books and magazines rely on design to catch the eye, hold the attention, and communicate information quickly and easily. Printed media generally use a combination of words and pictures. A designer makes them attractive by arranging them on the page, choosing different sizes and styles of type, and adding colour backgrounds and borders.

◤ SIMPLE SYMBOLS

Writing first developed in Sumeria (part of present-day Iraq) about 3400 BC, as a way of keeping records of farming, taxes, and trade. It used little pictures, called pictograms, to represent objects. Each pictogram was formed from wedge-shaped marks, made by pressing a reed pen into damp clay.

◤ PICTURE-WRITING

About 3000 BC, the ancient Egyptians invented hieroglyphs – writing that combined pictograms (pictures that portrayed objects) and ideograms (pictures that represented ideas). They were used for recording religious ideas.

◤ PRINTING PRESS

In about 1450, Johannes Gutenberg (c. 1400–68) invented a fast, low-cost method of printing. Metal letters were arranged to form a page of text, then inked and pressed against paper in a printing press like this one from 15th-century Florence.

◀ OVER THE AIR

Radio waves are an invisible form of electromagnetic energy. Italian scientist Guglielmo Marconi (1874–1937) pioneered their use as a means of communication. In 1897, he was the first person to send long-distance messages by radio, over a distance of 19 kilometres. In 1901, Marconi made the first 'wireless' transmission (as early radio was called) across the Atlantic. He was awarded the Nobel Prize for physics in 1909.

▶ THE SHAPE OF THE FUTURE?

The first television broadcasts were made in 1929. Early sets were disguised as pieces of decorative furniture. By 1949, when this 'Predicta' set was made, television was still a rare and expensive luxury, but the design of the 'Predicta' was streamlined and modern, rather than functional and hidden away. Today, there are television sets in most homes in the developed world.

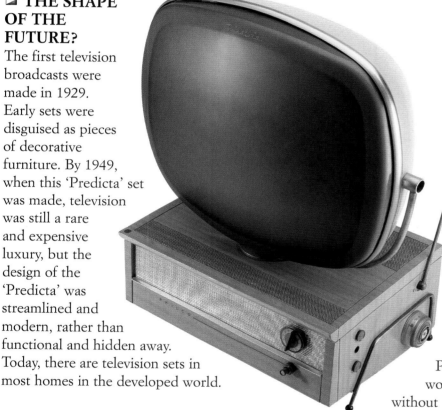

◢ HELLO?

Scottish-born inventor Alexander Graham Bell (1847–1922), who lived and worked in the United States, designed the first telephone in 1876. Telephones introduced a whole new way of communicating, based on a caller speaking to someone they could not see. People had to rely solely on words to convey information, without the help of body language.

TEXT MESSAGES AND EMAILS

In the past, people had to wait days or weeks to receive mail. Today, mobile phones (first widely available in the 1990s) and the Internet allow users to send and receive text messages worldwide in seconds.

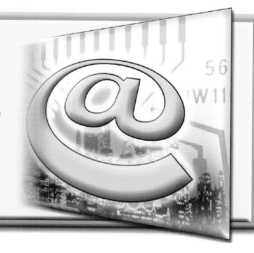

Sport

MANY sports and games developed as training for war. Men improved their strength, fitness and battlefield skills by running races, throwing javelins, boxing, wrestling, and shooting arrows. Games played on horseback, such as polo, were used to prepare cavalry fighters for long campaigns. Even games such as chess were useful training for army strategists – and spies! But sports and games were soon played for their own sake. Architects designed stadiums with facilities for players and spectators. During the 20th century, hi-tech designs and modern materials improved equipment such as tennis rackets and speed-bikes, allowing ever-faster speeds to be attained.

◪ OLYMPIC ARCH

Sports grounds, or stadiums, have existed for almost 3000 years. This stone archway marks the entrance to the main race track at Olympia, in Greece. According to tradition, the Olympic Games were first held at Olympia in 776 BC, originally to honour the Greek god Zeus.

◪ FAST, LIGHT AND UNSTEADY

Two-wheeled Roman chariots were fast, light, and easy to manoeuvre. They were originally designed to carry noblemen and army commanders into war, but were soon converted for use in one of Rome's most popular sports – chariot racing. Charioteers drove at breakneck speed around an oval arena, called a hippodrome.

◪ DRESSED TO WIN

During the late 20th century, new 'performance' clothes were designed to help athletes achieve their best. Made from artificial hi-tech fibres, they were tight, soft, light, stretchy, comfortable, and helped draw perspiration away from the skin.

☑ DESIGNED FOR DANGER

Players in some fast-moving sports, such as ice hockey (shown here) or football, run the risk of serious injury if they crash into one another or are hit by hard sticks or balls. For protection, they wear thick, padded clothing, tough boots and gloves, metal helmets and sometimes face masks as well.

THE BEST EQUIPMENT

In a sport like motor racing, the equipment can be as important as the driver's skill. Well-designed cars, like this Porsche built for US 'Indy' races, give their drivers an advantage. Drivers also rely on teams of expert technicians to keep their car in prime condition, or to mend it if it breaks down.

☑ BIG BY DESIGN

Sumo wrestling is an ancient Japanese sport that is still popular today. The men taking part are unusually big and extremely strong. Each wrestler normally weighs more than 160 kilograms, and tries to force his opponent to the ground by holds, trips, pushes and falls, in a series of bouts. The winner gains the most points, awarded by a referee.

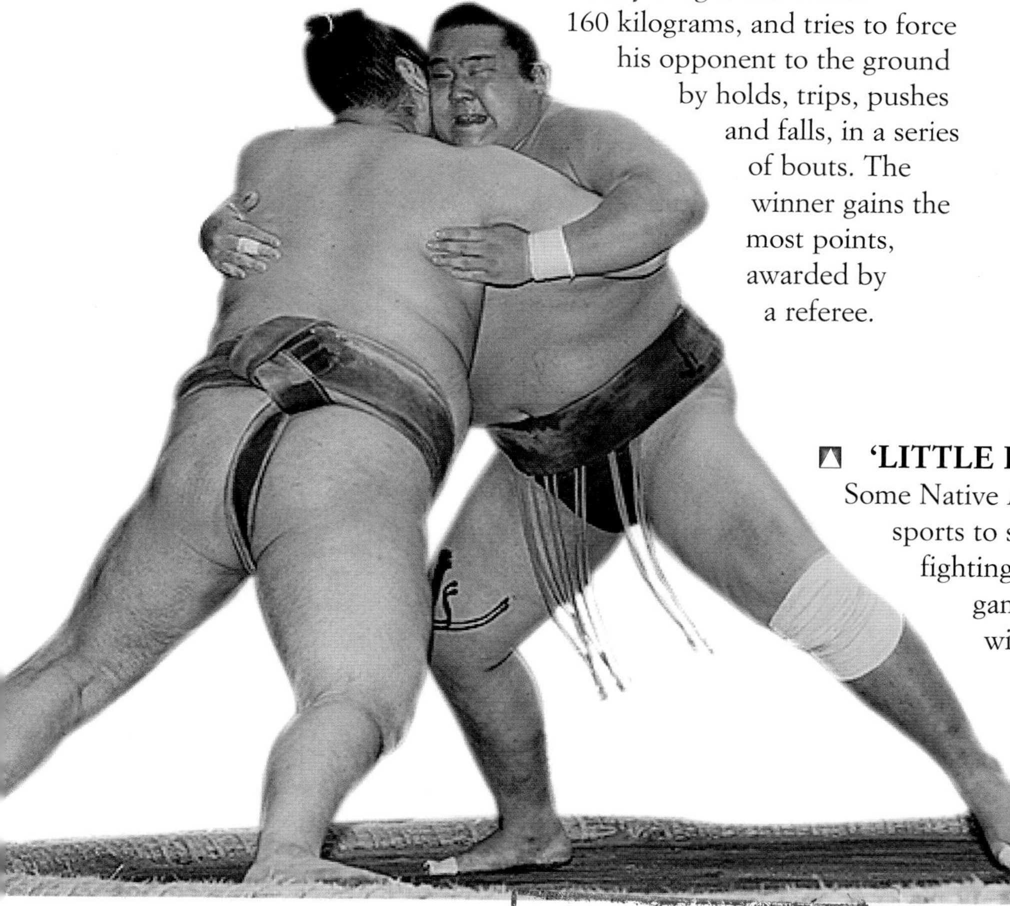

◩ 'LITTLE BROTHER OF WAR'

Some Native American peoples played sports to settle quarrels. Instead of fighting, whole villages joined in games like lacrosse – played with a ball and a stick with a net at one end. It was known as 'the little brother of war'.

Travel and transport

FOR most of history, travel was slow, difficult and often dangerous. Only people who had to travel, such as merchants, soldiers and sailors, made frequent long-distance journeys. But over the centuries, engineers have designed ever faster and more efficient vehicles, from the horse and cart to ships, trains, motor cars and aircraft. Since the mid-20th century, the rapid advances in vehicle design have enabled countless people to travel increasingly long distances, both for work and pleasure. Tourism is probably the world's largest industry now, and all over the world, whole resort villages are designed specially for tourists.

☑ SQUARE SAIL

The ancient Egyptians built the earliest-known ships in about 3000 BC. They were made from reeds and, like this slightly later wooden riverboat (c. 2500 BC), they had one square sail. The design of ships' sails did not change until the Middle Ages.

◄ RAILROAD REVOLUTION

The first steam locomotive was designed and built in England by engineer Richard Trevithick, in 1804. It was used to pull carriages along metal tracks. Railways transformed the way people lived. By 1845 (the date of this scene), trains carried factory-made goods to distant markets and food from the country to the fast-growing towns.

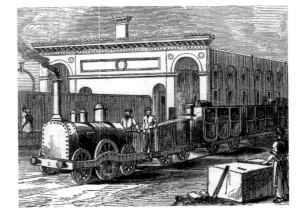

◄ THE FORCE OF THE WIND

The first European ship to have three masts was the caravel of the late 1400s. The next 350 years saw many changes in the design of ships, aimed at increasing their speed. By the 1840s, huge 'clipper' sailing ships like this one were the fastest wind-driven merchant ships ever built. They were able to sail from Asia to Europe, carrying tea and other goods, in less than 100 days.

STIRRUPS

Stirrups are loops with a flat base that are attached to a saddle by straps and support a rider's feet. Until they were invented in China, about AD 500, it was difficult to ride a galloping horse, or to throw a spear from horseback. Stirrups gave riders a strong 'platform' on which to stand.

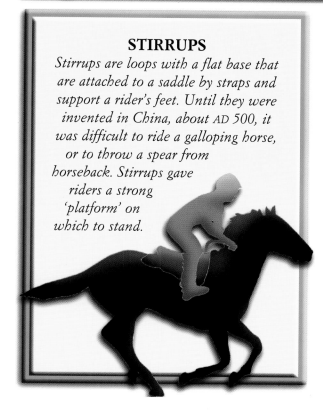

◪ TOP SPEED

The first petrol engine, or internal combustion engine, was designed by German inventors Daimler and Benz in 1885. In 1903, the early Rolls-Royce car (above) held the world record for speed. It could travel for short distances at 134 kilometres per hour. Today, cars provide fast, convenient transportation for millions of people, but they also cause serious environmental pollution.

◲ THE JET AGE

Jet engines, like those on this Boeing 747, work by pushing out a stream of exhaust gases very fast at the rear. This drives the plane forward through the air. The first jet engines were designed in the 1930s by British engineer Frank Whittle. Since the 1960s, fast jet travel has enabled many people to travel abroad for their holidays. Super-fast jet planes are also used by many armed forces for bombing, air attack and reconnaissance.

◩ ANIMAL LOADS

Before the 20th century, people relied on animals to provide power for transport, and to carry heavy loads. Horses, donkeys and mules pulled carriages and carts or were laden with panniers, or baskets, and camels carried heavy loads across deserts. Animal transport was often slow, and could be dangerous. Frightened animals might bolt, throwing off baggage and riders, while sickly animals could die, leaving travellers stranded.

Risk and danger

RISK and danger are part of human life. Some people, like airline test pilots or movie stunt actors, take risks as a way of earning a living. Others have tried to protect themselves from danger by designing and making all kinds of special devices. These range from magic charms and special clothes to protective gadgets built into machines. For some, like emergency aid workers or firefighters, facing risks and dangers is an unpleasant, but necessary, side to helping people in need.

A few people add risks to their 'design for living' by practicing dangerous sports, such as mountain climbing. For them, facing up to death is a way of feeling more alive.

◨ LUCKY CHARM

Many peoples around the world have carried an amulet, or lucky charm to protect them from danger. In ancient Egypt, amulets often showed a scarab, or dung beetle. Scarabs roll a ball of dung over the ground, which reminded the Egyptians of the life-giving Sun rolling across the sky.

◧ DRESSED TO FACE DEATH

In the 16th and 17th centuries, European doctors treating patients with deadly diseases, such as bubonic plague, dressed in unusual protective clothing. They wore long cloaks, leather gloves, close-fitting hats and pointed masks like birds' beaks, stuffed with antiseptic herbs and spices.

WARNING LIGHT

Before modern electronic navigation aids, ships relied on lighthouses to warn them of dangerous rocks. Each lighthouse flashed its own signal pattern, so that sailors could identify their location.

◨ UNDER THE WAVES

Deep-sea divers perform essential tasks in many industries, such as offshore oil and gas drilling, salvaging wrecked ships and their cargoes, and making underwater surveys to help geologists. They also work for the police and coast guards, helping in rescue operations. This submersible ship is designed to carry divers safely from support ships on the surface to their work on the seabed.

DANGEROUS WORK

For movie stunt actors, taking risks is a way of earning a living. All kinds of devices have been designed to make their acts look more dangerous than they really are. A jump or fall from a building, for example, may be less far than it appears on camera, and will be cushioned by an air mattress.

OUT OF THIS WORLD

Astronauts face all kinds of risks in space. Inside their spaceships, they breathe a special mixture of gases. Outside, working in space, they have to wear heavy protective suits, which provide them with oxygen to breathe, supply heat to stop them freezing to death and protect their bodies from harmful radiation.

FIRE!

Firefighters are trained to face danger in order to help save others in emergencies. They rely on special clothing, like this fireproof suit, to survive in extreme conditions. Made from the latest highly resistant materials, it insulates the skin from excessive heat. The multi-layered face-mask is also designed to prevent hot ash from entering the firefighter's mouth and nose.

Weapons and warfare

WEAPONS are designed to kill or to inflict serious injuries. Over the centuries, engineers have designed fearsome machines for attack or defence in war. Some were adaptations of inventions first designed for peaceful purposes. Barbed wire, for example, was originally designed as a fence for cattle, but during World War I (1914–18) it was used to entangle thousands of soldiers on the battlefields of Europe. Other wartime inventions were later modified for peaceful functions. Gunpowder, invented in China as a weapon in about AD 1000, was soon used in small amounts to create fireworks, which have delighted people at special celebrations ever since.

◪ EXPLOSIVE!

Gunpowder was first used in Europe from about AD 1300. Early cannons fired heavy stone or metal balls at defensive walls. At first they were hardly more effective than weapons that catapulted rocks, but gradually their range improved and they could be placed farther back from the enemy.

◩ SIEGE ENGINES

In medieval Europe (c. AD 1000–1500), huge 'siege engines' were used to attack the defensive stone walls of castles and cities. Some were designed to smash holes in stonework, or to hurl rocks over the walls. Others were shaped like tall, movable towers. They carried soldiers close to the castle, to give them a better chance of climbing inside.

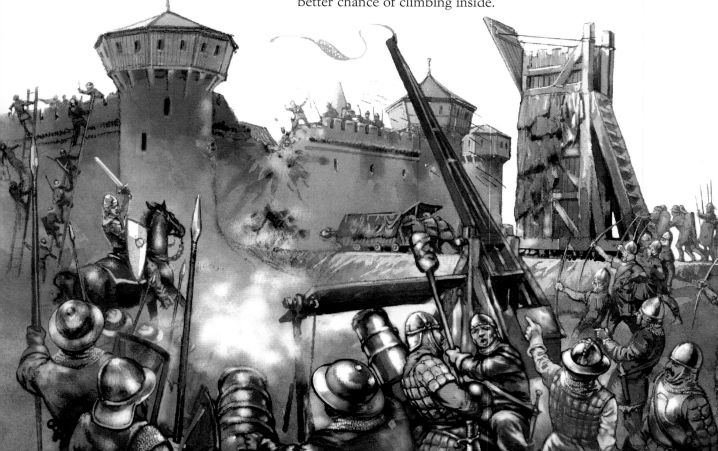

◢ MACHINE GUNS

The first machine guns were
invented in 1862 by
American inventors
Richard Gatling
and Wilson Agar.
They were designed to
fire a continuous stream of
bullets much more quickly
than any hand-held gun.
Machine guns were
expensive, but gave any army
who owned them a great
advantage over their enemies.

◨ INVISIBLE?

During the late 20th century, new
aircraft like this B2 'stealth' bomber were
designed to be invisible to radar- or heat-
detecting devices. Able to fly unobserved over
enemy territory, they can carry out precision
attacks on targets using laser-guided bombs.
But the unusual design
of 'stealth' aircraft makes
them both difficult to
fly and expensive to
operate and maintain.

TRENCHES

*During World War I
(1914–18), millions of
men fought in the
trenches of Belgium and
France. Trenches were
deep slits dug into the
ground. Although
designed as places to hide
from enemy fire, they
became death wtraps.*

◪ FLYING BOMBS

Missiles are powerful 'flying bombs', first used in
1942. Modern missiles are designed to
destroy a wide range of targets. They can
be fitted with radar or infrared
equipment to steer themselves,
or can be guided by human
operators. Some carry
nuclear warheads.

◧ UNSTOPPABLE

Tanks were first used in
battle in France in 1917.
The 'caterpillar' tracks
that carry them along are
designed to cope with
the most difficult terrain,
and can flatten obstacles
that would stop wheeled
vehicles in their tracks.
Armour plating protects
the soldiers inside.

Worship

SOME of the world's most beautiful buildings, finest works of art and greatest treasures were designed for use in worship. Rich patrons provided the money to pay for religious objects, while artists and architects lavished time, skill and the best materials on creations designed for religious use. Why did they do this at a time when many people around them were desperately poor? Partly, they wanted to provide a splendid home for their god or gods. To show that a holy site was special, religious leaders made sure that it was clean, beautiful, richly decorated, and kept in good repair. Sometimes patrons and artists wanted to create a memorial to themselves, or to leave a lasting monument for others to admire.

◥ MAGICAL ART

In ancient Egypt, art was believed to have a magic power that could keep a person's spirit alive. This tomb painting is of the Sun god Re (or Ra), the mythical first king of Egypt.

◥ PLACE OF BLESSINGS

For Hindus, a temple, or *mandir*, is a very special place. It is designed to house a *murti* – a holy statue of a goddess or god. Visitors to the temple bring sweets, fruit or flowers to offer to the god, and are blessed by temple priests in return. This Hindu temple is on the island of Bali, Indonesia.

◩ SKILFULLY CRAFTED FROM MUD

The magnificent mosque in Djenne, in central Mali, north Africa, is the largest mud-brick building in the world. Built in 1906, its design was based on that of the great 13th-century mosque that stood on the site for about 600 years. Every year after the rainy season, the smooth layer of mud that covers the bricks has to be repaired.

HOLY HOMES

The ancient town of Çatal Hüyük, in Turkey, dates from about 6000 BC. Evidence suggests that many of the houses were built as shrines – they had ox skulls fixed to the walls, and many bodies were found buried under the floors. No one knows who was worshipped there, but it may have been a mother-goddess.

DIVINE DECORATIONS

Distinctive onion-shaped domes decorate Orthodox churches all over Russia, including St. Basil's Cathedral in Moscow. The Orthodox Church is one of the four main divisions of Christianity. It parted from the other three soon after AD 1000. Orthodox churches contain icons – holy portraits of Jesus, the Virgin Mary, and Christian saints.

GOD IS HERE

To Jewish people, lighted candles burning in a *menorah* – a multi-branched candlestick – are a sign of God's presence. Traditionally, a great golden *menorah* was kept constantly burning in the ancient Jewish temple in Jerusalem. Today, many Jewish people light candles at the yearly festival of Hanukkah, and on other special days.

PILGRIMS

In the past, many Christians travelled long distances to places where saints' remains were displayed in specially designed caskets called reliquaries. The pilgrims believed that seeing, or touching, the remains would bring blessings, and might even cure illness.

Glossary

ALLOY
A metallic substance made from a mixture of two or more metals, or from a metal mixed with other non-metallic elements, examples being brass, bronze and steel.

AMPHITHEATRE
A circular or oval building with rows of seats which rise from an arena, where performances take place for an audience.

ARCHITECT
A person who design buildings.

ASTRONAUTS
From the Greek words for 'space sailor', people who are trained to travel in space.

BACTERIA
Tiny, single-celled living things found almost everywhere, and which have many ways of life – some are important as recyclers of nutrients in the natural world, while others known as germs cause diseases.

BAR CODES
Patterns of wide and narrow bands found on labels, goods and packaging, especially in supermarkets, and which carry information such as the price of the goods. They are read by a laser beam at the check-out.

BEAM-CRANE
A machine designed to lift and move heavy loads by means of a hook hanging from a rod, or boom, using a system of ropes and pulleys. The boom is moved along a beam, which is supported by an upright pier at each end.

BLACKSMITH
A craftsperson who shapes and joins iron and other metals, by heating them and hitting them with a hammer against an anvil,

a type of metal block. Blacksmiths make many metal items, from tools to horseshoes.

BROADCAST
To scatter or spread something over a wide area – today this word usually refers to the spreading of information, news or knowledge usually by radio or television.

CENTENARY
The 100th anniversary of an event, or the celebration of it.

CERAMICS
Objects that are made by shaping and firing (heating) clay or similar materials, at very high temperatures, so they become hard and brittle.

CHARIOTS
Wheeled vehicles, usually horse-drawn, invented about 5000 years ago for fast travel and particularly warfare. Soldiers, especially Romans, raced chariots to show their skills and bravery.

CONCRETE
Hard, strong building material made from mixing aggregate (sand and gravel), water and cement (chalk and clay which has been ground, mixed together and burned).

CURRENCY
The money – notes and coins – that is particular to a country, that often shows national symbols.

DIGITAL
Digital images are recorded and displayed, not as continuous areas of shape and colour, but as codes of numbers, or digits, which can be shown as special points called pixels on a TV or on a computer screen.

ELECTROMAGNETIC ENERGY
Energy which travels in waves which are partly electrical and partly magnetic, and which include radio and television waves, microwaves, infra red, light rays, ultra violet and X-rays.

ENGRAVING
A printing technique where a pattern or image is cut or engraved into a metal or wooden plate, ink is rubbed on, and then the plate is pressed onto paper.

FOSSIL FUELS
Substances such as oil, coal and natural gas formed millions of years ago, when plants and animals died and became buried and preserved, and which are now burned to produce heat.

GLADIATORS
Men trained to fight each other or wild animals and provide a bloodthirsty spectacle, especially for the huge audiences attending the arenas in ancient Rome.

GUNPOWDER
A mixture of chemicals such as potassium nitrate, charcoal and sulphur, which explodes when ignited by a spark. It is used in fireworks and weapons.

HIEROGLYPHS
The system of writing that uses small pictures to represent words, syllables, or sounds, and which was invented and used by, for example, the ancient Egyptians, for religious texts.

ICONS
Sacred images from Christianity such as Christ, Mary, a saint or a scene from the Bible – sculpted or painted onto wooden panels and used as a centrepiece for prayer and worship.

INDY RACES
The form of motor racing where the cars race round an oval circuit. The main races are at Indianapolis, USA, from where the name 'Indy' is taken.

INFORMATION TECHNOLOGY
The system for storing, retrieving and sending information, especially in electronic form using computers, fibre optic and wire cables, telecommunications' networks, microwaves, radio waves, satellites and the Internet.

INTERNAL COMBUSTION ENGINE
A machine which burns or combusts fuel within an enclosed space, usually called a cylinder, to produce expanding gases which provide the pressure used to move a piston or turn a rotor.

LASER
A special high-energy light of a single pure colour.

MASON
A person who builds or works with stone.

MEDIA
Plural for 'medium' – the substance, method or means by which something is carried or happens. The term is used for the ways by which information is communicated, such as television, radio, newspapers, magazines, photographs and the Internet.

MEDIEVAL
Usually referring to the Middle or Dark Ages, a 1000-year period in history, which generally began at the end of the Roman era, around 400 AD, and ended with the Renaissance, around 1400 AD.

MOSAICS
Decorative patterns or pictures made by arranging tiny pieces of coloured glass, tiles, or stones, often bedding them into cement or mortar to be firmly held.

MOSQUE
A building where Muslims (followers of Islam) meet to worship, pray, and listen to readings from the Holy Book, the *Qu'ran*.

NOBEL PRIZES
Six international awards given annually to people who have made great achievements in physics, chemistry, physiology or medicine, literature, economics and the promotion of peace. They are named after the Swedish industrialist Alfred Nobel.

PATRON
A rich person, or benefactor, who pays, gives gifts to, or otherwise assists a poorer but talented person such as a musician, artist, composer or actor.

POLLUTION
Anything which disturbs, contaminates or harms nature or the environment, in any way – chemicals, noise, heat, radioactivity, visual eyesores and so on.

PREHISTORIC
The time from when the Earth began, or from a certain creation time, to when written records began, usually regarded as about 12,000–10,000 years ago.

PYRAMID
A structure with a straight-edged base and sloping sides, and which was usually used for religious purposes, such as the tombs of a god-kings or pharaohs in Egypt, or for sacrifices in the Americas.

RADAR
A system of scanning the surrounding area by sending out pulses of high-frequency radio waves, receiving their reflections or echoes when they bounce off objects, and analyzing the reflections to work out the direction and distance of objects.

RADIATION
The passage or transfer of energy, either in the form of waves – especially electromagnetic energy such as radio waves or light rays – or as tiny particles such as radioactivity.

STEAM ENGINE
A machine that burns fuel to heat water and turn it to steam, which expands to produce pressure useful for driving machines such as pumps or locomotives.

STONE AGE
The period of human history, broadly up to about 10,000 years ago, when people used tools made of natural materials such as wood, bone, rock and stone, but not of processed materials such as metals.

TEMPLE
Building used for prayer and worship of a god, goddess or similar revered person, or regarded as the place of residence of that person, or which has some similar religious importance.

TEXTILES
A term originally used only for cloth made by weaving (passing crosswise threads, or weft, between lengthways threads, or warp), but now used for fabric made by any method.

VISUAL POLLUTION
The description of something that is unpleasant to look at, or that spoils the look of something else, such as a certain buildings within a city.

X-RAYS
Electromagnetic energy with very short waves of great power. The term also refers to pictures produced on photographic film when X-rays are shone at or though an object, such as the human body.

Index

ACKNOWLEDGEMENTS